URBAN ATROPHY
MID-ATLANTIC

DAN HAGA

Schiffer
Publishing Ltd®

4880 Lower Valley Road Atglen, Pennsylvania 19310

ACKNOWLEDGMENTS

I would like to say a special thank you to all those who helped make *Urban Atrophy* possible, including: my wife Samantha, my parents Danny and Carol Haga, Matt Haga, Dan Ayers, Matt Palmer, Steve Corley, Thomas Otto, Tom White, Chris Dupler, Larry McAvoy, Rick Pendelton, John Howard, Natalie Bock, Dave Vos, Charlotte Taboso, David Edwards, Edward Hopkins, Janice Bowen, David Knipp, Samantha Cook, and Elaine Scott.

Type set in Garamond Pro and Bailey Sans
ISBN: 978-0-7643-3738-3
Printed in China

Schiffer Books are available at special discounts for bulk purchases for sales promotions or premiums. Special editions, including personalized covers, corporate imprints, and excerpts can be created in large quantities for special needs. For more information contact the publisher:

Published by Schiffer Publishing Ltd.
4880 Lower Valley Road
Atglen, PA 19310
Phone: (610) 593-1777; Fax: (610) 593-2002
E-mail: Info@schifferbooks.com

For the largest selection of fine reference books on this and related subjects, please visit our website at **www.schifferbooks.com**
We are always looking for people to write books on new and related subjects. If you have an idea for a book please contact us at the above address.

This book may be purchased from the publisher.
Include $5.00 for shipping.
Please try your bookstore first.
You may write for a free catalog.

In Europe, Schiffer books are distributed by
Bushwood Books
6 Marksbury Ave.
Kew Gardens
Surrey TW9 4JF England
Phone: 44 (0) 20 8392 8585; Fax: 44 (0) 20 8392 9876
E-mail: info@bushwoodbooks.co.uk
Website: www.bushwoodbooks.co.uk

CONTENTS

INTRODUCTION

As a kid, I was always fascinated with exploring the property I grew up on. I would search the woods for old building foundations and relics, following trails and railroad tracks to see where they led. I was always curious—what laid a little farther? or what is on the other side of that fence? It wasn't until age 25, when I received a camera as a wedding gift, that I began documenting my adventures. I teamed up with a long time friend and created the *Urban Atrophy* website (www.urbanatrophy.com). The website focused on photo galleries and bits of history that we gathered from the locations we visited. Word quickly spread and before we knew it we were being interviewed by television stations and written about in the local newspapers; then people all over the world were requesting to use our work in books, magazines, and various other publications. At that point I had become addicted to exploring and photographing places that were abandoned and off-limits. I wanted each adventure to be bigger and better than the previous. Being in an abandoned place was like being in another world, a surreal dream where people just disappeared and left everything behind. I knew these places were once crowded and noisy with people, but now these buildings lie silent and dying—power plants, jails, churches, sanitariums, whatever it was. I couldn't help but to wonder: What did the men running this machinery like to joke about as the asbestos-filled air ripped years of life away from them? What did the prisoner in this cell think as he sat on death row, and what had he done to get there? How many children passed through this morgue? What were the worst sins people begged forgiveness for at this altar? There is just so much more to these places than concrete and rotting wood. I strive to capture the emotions of these locations with my photography so that I'm able to share them with people that might not have ever seen them or known they existed otherwise.

MEDICINE

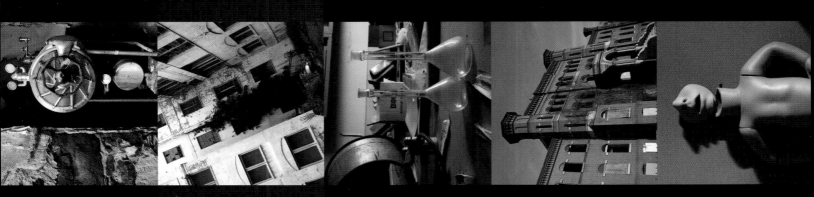

St. Elizabeth's Hospital

Washington, DC

Located in Southeast Washington, DC, St. Elizabeths Hospital rests on a bluff with an enchanting view overlooking the Potomac and Anacostia Rivers. Established in 1855, the hospital was originally named the Government Hospital for the Insane. The hospital's mission was "to provide the most humane care and enlightened curative treatment of the insane of the Army, Navy, and District of Columbia." During the Civil War, wounded soldiers treated within the facility were reluctant to divulge the fact that they were being housed in an insane asylum—an understandable reaction given the building's rather heartless title. Soldiers reverted to the colonial name of the land where the hospital was built—St. Elizabeths. Congress officially changed the hospital's name to St. Elizabeths in 1916. By the 1940s, the hospital complex covered an area of over 300 acres and housed nearly 7,000 patients. It was the first, and only, federal mental facility with a national reach.

The property's now-untrodden soil also claims a Civil War cemetery where hundreds of Union and Confederate soldiers alike, whom had spent their last days at St. Elizabeths, lay at rest. While only a few hundred graves are marked, with superstition set aside, it is believed that thousands of patients are buried on the property.

Partitioned by Martin Luther King Jr. Avenue, the campus is split into two sides. The west side, currently owned by the federal government, is the older of the two. Accompanying the typical problems associated with aging buildings, medicine and equipment shortages also plagued the west campus. Eventually, all of the patients were transferred to the newer east campus.

As it sat weathered and attended only by time itself, the west campus crumbled into a state of great disrepair. The main building was designated a National Historic Landmark, preventing it from being demolished. With rehabilitation and reuse costs estimated in the hundreds of millions, private developers showed no interest in breathing life back into the historic west side of St. Elizabeths. In 2007 the federal government stepped in and announced that it would be spending the billions required to rehabilitate the main building in an effort to consolidate dozens of individual offices. The master plan is for this to become the headquarters for the Department of Homeland Security (DHS). Phase one of this plan has the US Coast Guard occupying new headquarters on the site in 2013 and the rest of DHS moving in 2014.

Built in 1907, Victor Cullen, originally known as the State Sanatorium, was the first state-funded tuberculosis sanatorium in Maryland. The administration building (pictured here) once boasted eight detached wings, which were designed to isolate patients in an environment with maximum ventilation in all weather conditions. As the need for tuberculosis treatment subsided, the wings were demolished and the facility was transformed into a state hospital only to be changed once again, in 1965, into a reform school for boys. While many of the original buildings are now sealed up and unused, there is still an active juvenile treatment program that utilizes a newer detention center on the property.

Hebrew Orphan Asylum

Baltimore, MD

Fate played cruel irony on the Hebrew Orphan Asylum which now stands like one of its own, neglected in a mostly vacated West Baltimore neighborhood. The building—established as the Hebrew Orphan Asylum in 1872—was originally believed to have been the old Baltimore County Almshouse (a hospital reserved for those of insufficient income who could not attain private medical care). Funded by wealthy Jewish families and surrounded by farmland, the Orphan Asylum only operated for a short time before being destroyed by fire in 1874. The building was soon rebuilt though, again, largely assisted by contributions made from the Hebrews of Baltimore. With the help of The Hebrew Ladies Aid Society, hundreds of orphans were cared for in the structure until lack of funding forced the orphanage to close its doors in 1923. In 1924 the site reopened as the West Baltimore General Hospital and expanded with various new buildings. Later the facility became the Lutheran Hospital. It has been empty since 1989 and was recently designated as a National Historic site.

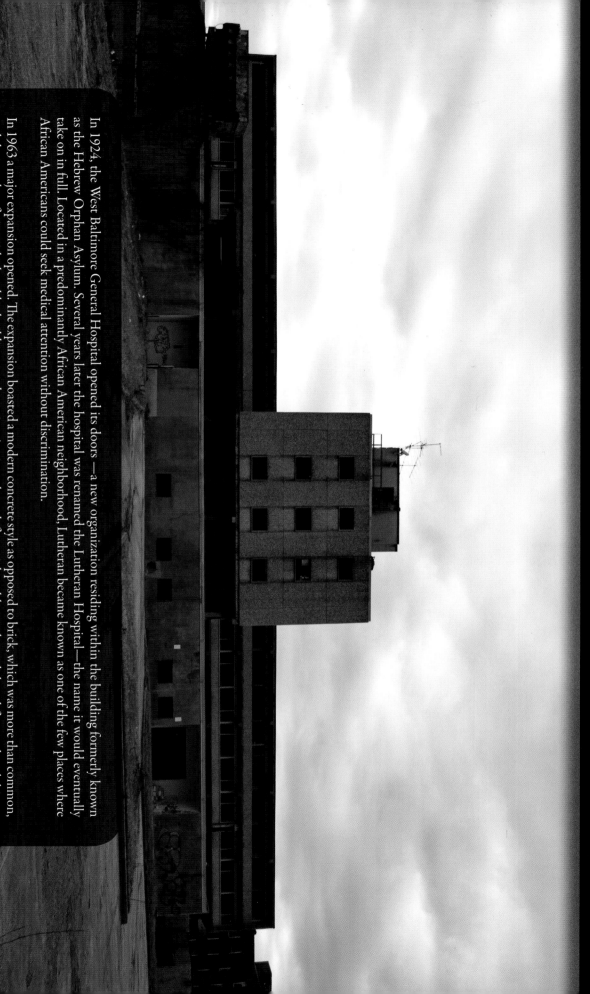

Lutheran Hospital

Baltimore, MD

In 1924, the West Baltimore General Hospital opened its doors —a new organization residing within the building formerly known as the Hebrew Orphan Asylum. Several years later the hospital was renamed the Lutheran Hospital—the name it would eventually take on in full. Located in a predominantly African American neighborhood, Lutheran became known as one of the few places where African Americans could seek medical attention without discrimination.

In 1963 a major expansion opened. The expansion boasted a modern concrete style as opposed to brick, which was more than common, and designed to fit in with the older buildings used on site. As time elapsed, financial problems plagued the edifice, and with bigger and better hospital facilities popping up over the city, it was forced to close down in 1989. After sitting vacant for nearly twenty years, Coppin State University acquired the property and demolished the main hospital. Even with a new claim to the property, the original Orphan Asylum building was recently designated a National Historic site and saved from demolition.

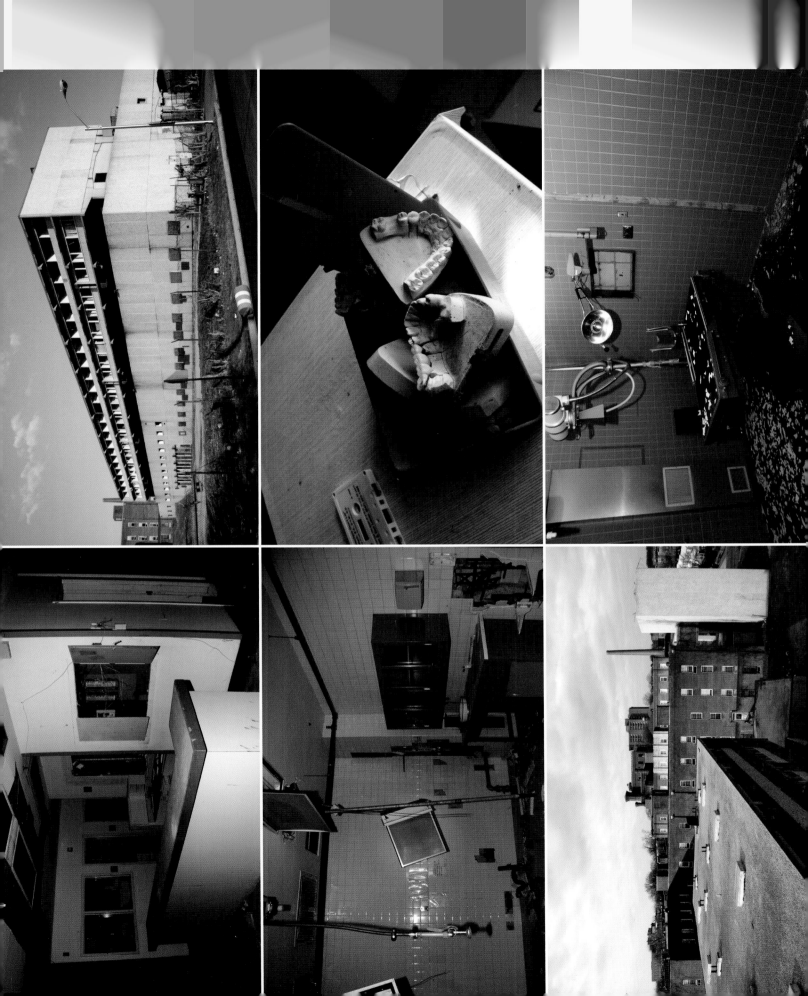

Henryton Center

Marriottsvile, MD

Henryton State Hospital is situated in a heavily wooded, steeply sloped, rural area in central Maryland. The facility was originally established in the 1920s as a tuberculosis hospital serving the African American population. Henryton was reformed in 1962 as a facility serving the developmentally disabled population (i.e., mental retardation), and finally ceased its functions in 1985. It has been vacant since closing. Today, Maryland State Police occasionally take advantage of the facility to train police dogs and demonstrate how to detect scents, conduct searches, etc. The property is presently on the market but struggling to sell due to environmental concerns and the historical value of several buildings, which prevents them from being torn down.

Unfortunately, the desolate site has become a popular target for metal scrappers, vandals, and arsons. Much of what you see in these photos, including the old theatre, has since been destroyed by fire.

The Henryton campus consists of eighteen buildings, with a total of 228,000 square feet. It is located on a vast 46-acre plot in the middle of a State Park. The main buildings at Henryton include three connecting multi-story structures, built between the 1920s and 1940, expanding over approximately 119,000 square feet. The main hospital building is the original tuberculosis hospital. Two additions were built and renovations were made to the original building between the time of the original construction and 1940. There are also five support buildings located nearby. These were built between 1936 and 1952 and contain approximately 96,000 square feet. Seven small maintenance buildings and sheds scattered throughout the campus were constructed between the 1920s and 1940 and have a total of 8,000 square feet of space. Lastly, there are three other maintenance buildings which were constructed between 1957 and 1960.

Rosewood Center

Owings Mills, MD

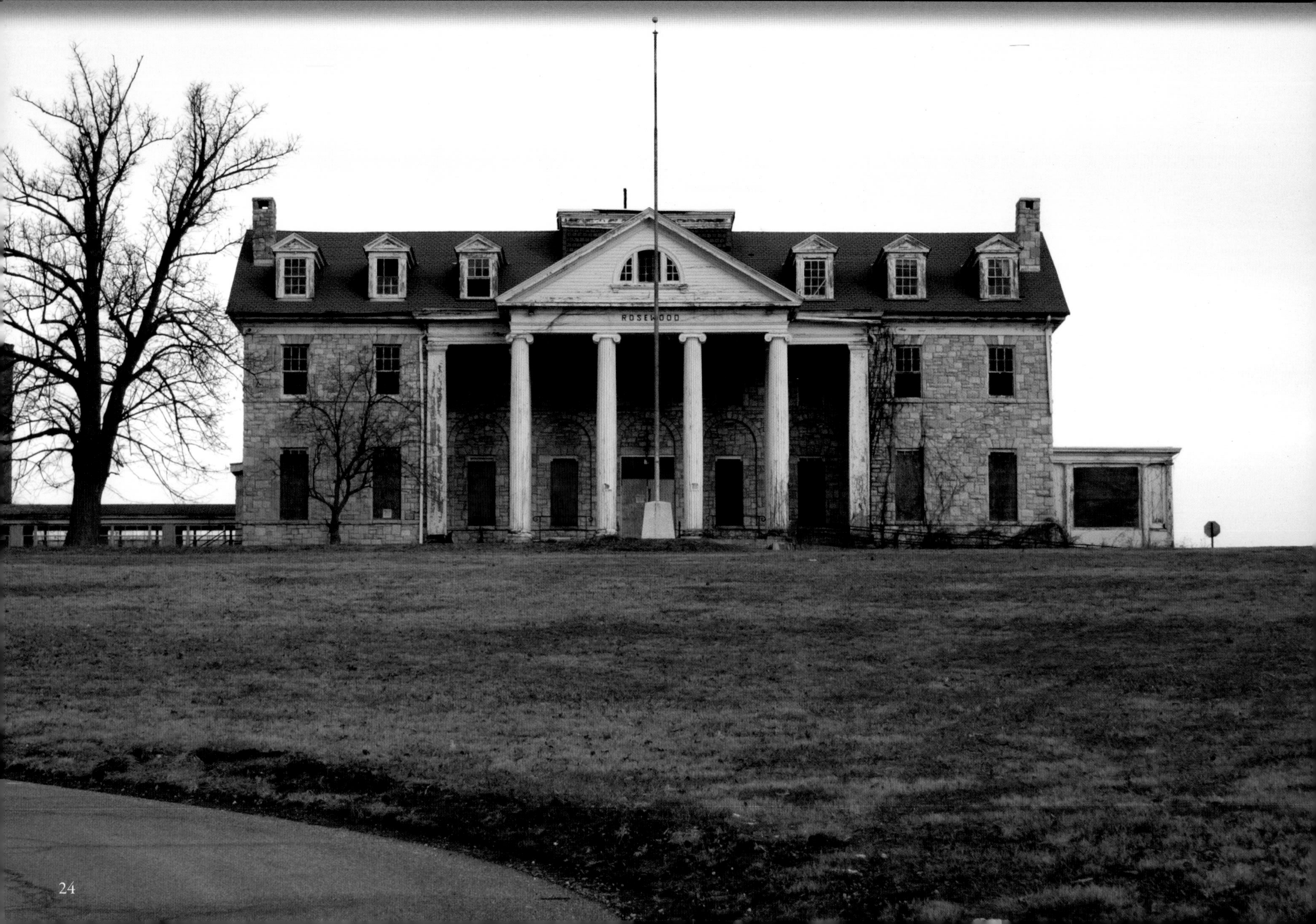

The Rosewood training school was established in the late 1800s to treat the developmentally disabled. To this day, a large safe sits in the basement of the school, packed with reports of physical abuse, sexual abuse, neglect, and unsanitary living conditions. Needless to say, the school acquired a disturbing reputation. Clearly, even the recently active portion of the facility had been operating at an unacceptable level for far too long. State inspections of the facility confirm finding reports stashed in the basement: "deteriorating housing...unsafe conditions...patient-on-patient violence...substandard medical..." were among the more common complaints detailed.

In early 2008, an announcement was made that the Rosewood Center was to be closed down and patients relocated. The majority of the photos shown here are of the Administration building, which was completely destroyed by arson in 1996. The future of the site is currently unknown but the neighboring Stevenson University is showing interest in the property for campus expansion.

DC General Hospital is part of a much larger campus known as Reservation 13. The Reservation 13 facility also includes the DC Jail and Correctional Treatment Facility, medical clinics, various medical offices, and work spaces. The main buildings of DC General Hospital were constructed in the 1930s and 1940s but history can be traced back to the mid 1800s, when the site was known as Hospital Square and home to the Washington Asylum.

Currently, most of Reservation 13 is vacant and the DC government is seeking a developer to transform the 67 acre site into a mix of offices, health facilities, housing, and park land.

MEDICINE DC General Hospital

Crownsville Hospital

Crownsville, MD

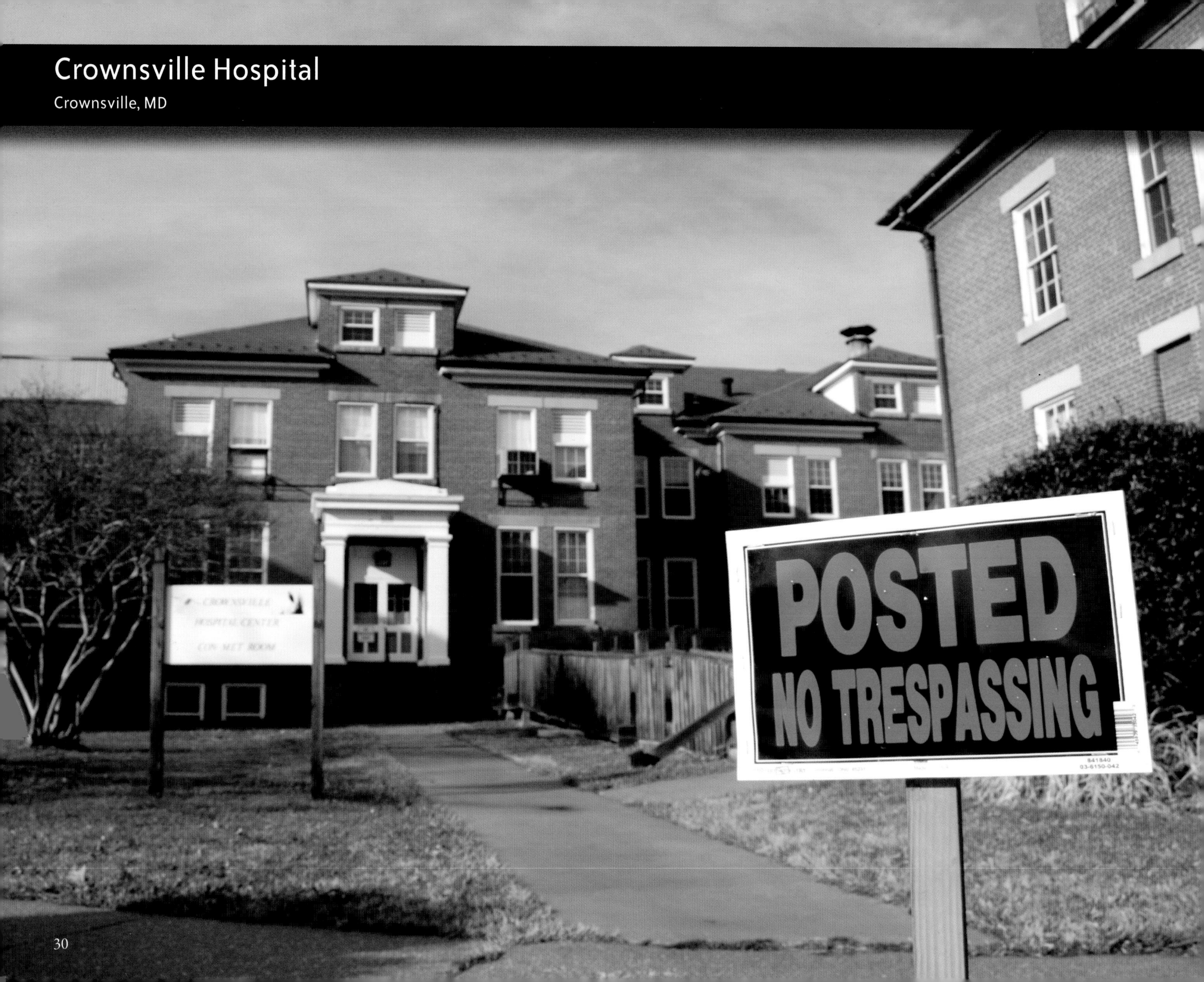

Established in 1910, The Crownsville Hospital Center was originally known as "The Hospital for the Negro Insane of Maryland." Initially, patients were kept in old farm buildings and used to help build roads and harvest crops until the first hospital building was built in 1912. Crownsville has seen more than its fair share of hard times—patients were struck with smallpox, scarlet fever, and tuberculosis—all of which swiftly spread due to a lack of effort to isolate the infected patients. Later, overcrowded and understaffed, the hospital was labeled "Maryland's Shame" by the local media. Men, women, and children were forced to dwell in the very same wards that were packed with criminally insane, mentally ill, and diseased patients. There are many rumors of patient abuse, neglect, and other horror stories from Crownsville, but by the time the facility closed in 2004 this shadowy history was largely forgotten.

Glenn Dale Hospital

Glenn Dale, MD

Glenn Dale Hospital is a sprawling, abandoned complex surrounded by park land and residential communities near Washington, DC. It was originally built in the 1930s as a tuberculosis hospital, and then later born-again into a general hospital and secondarily as a mental hospital. In 1982 the hospital closed down, leaving behind the massive buildings as well as many smaller surrounding structures that remain unused and abandoned to this day. The current owner is seeking historic designation, hoping the associated tax breaks will encourage the adaptive reuse of the buildings.

Sydenham Hospital
Baltimore, MD

Built in the early 1900s at Lake Montebello, the Sydenham Hospital was originally used to isolate and treat communicable diseases such as diphtheria, measles, scarlet fever, smallpox, and chicken pox. With the modern revolution in antibiotics — beginning with the discovery of penicillin in 1928 and again the commercial availability of prontosil in 1932 — the need for a specific hospital to treat infectious diseases dwindled. As a result, Sydenham Hospital was closed in 1949 and converted to serve other health and rehabilitation needs. Parts of the campus remain in use, but many of the original buildings have been vacant for numerous years.

Washington, DC

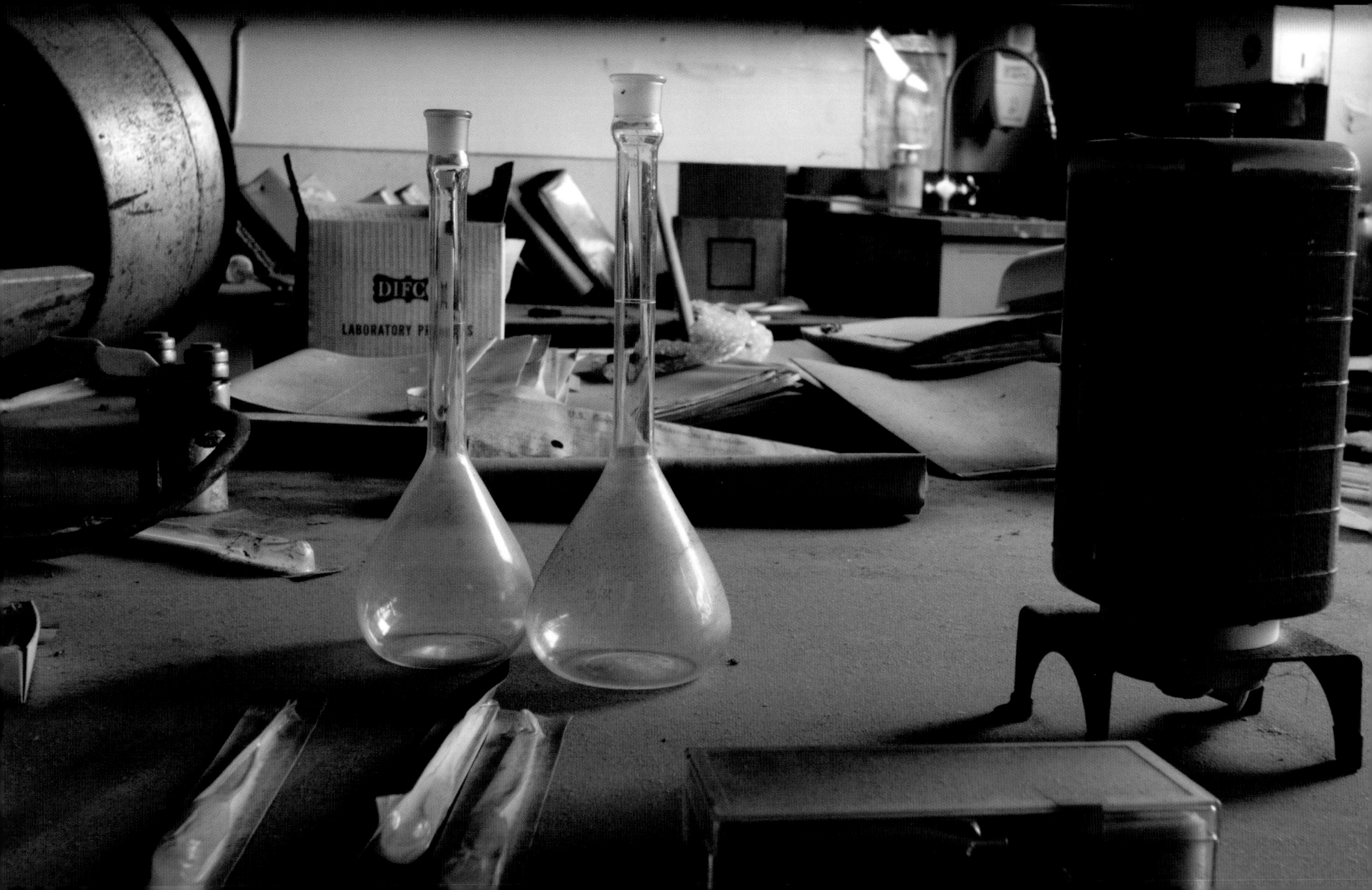

The DC Village, known as the Home for the Aged and the Infirm, was opened in 1906 in the Blue Plains area of DC. The nursing home campus embodied a five-story infirmary, ample central building, auditorium, chapel, and a vast complex of cottages. In addition to the elderly, the center also accepted and treated mental patients who were refused admittance by Forest Haven and St. Elizabeths Hospital. Throughout most of the facility's challenging lifetime it was burdened with reports of poor living conditions, abuse, neglect, malnutrition, and worse. In 1995 the Justice Department reported findings of 37 preventable deaths at the institution. The DC Village was closed down, only to reopen as a homeless shelter, which would also later be closed for overcrowding and "inhumane" conditions. The Washington Metropolitan Area Transit Authority (WMATA) purchased the property for $6.45 million from the District and plans to build a new bus garage on the site. The infirmary has been demolished and construction has started on the first phase of the garage which will house 114 Metrobuses. A second phase could increase capacity to 250 buses. The facility will also dispense compressed natural gas to buses. The garage will replace the 72-year-old Southeastern Bus Garage.

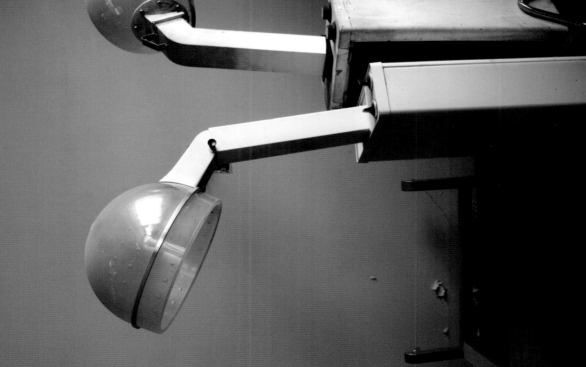

Springfield Hospital

Sykesville, MD

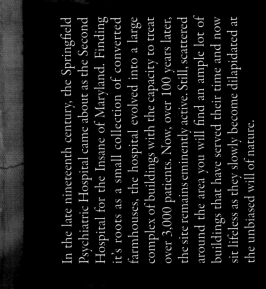

In the late nineteenth century, the Springfield Psychiatric Hospital came about as the Second Hospital for the Insane of Maryland. Finding it's roots as a small collection of converted farmhouses, the hospital evolved into a large complex of buildings with the capacity to treat over 3,000 patients. Now, over 100 years later, the site remains eminently active. Still, scattered around the area you will find an ample lot of buildings that have served their time and now sit lifeless as they slowly become dilapidated at the unbiased will of nature.

Fort Howard VAMC

Fort Howard, MD

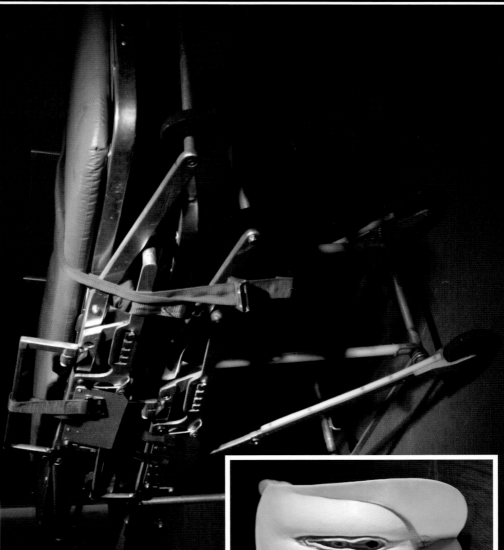

This hospital was built around 1940 on the post garrison area of Fort Howard. The rehabilitation facility, which had 154 hospital beds, also provided rehabilitation medicine, geriatric medicine, substance abuse rehabilitation, subacute care, and outpatient services. It also operated a 47-bed nursing home care unit that was closed in 1996 with the opening of the new nursing home in Baltimore. Many of the other services that were available here have been transferred elsewhere.

Of the many structures on site, all of them are abandoned with the exception of the out-patient clinic, grounds crew building, and the security building at the front gate. Plans are in the works to create a veterans' retirement community on the old campus so it may not last much longer in its current condition before demolition and rebuilding begins.

Spring Grove Hospital

Catonsville, MD

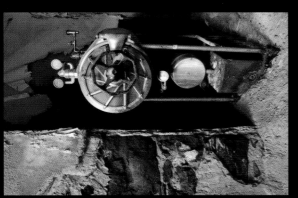

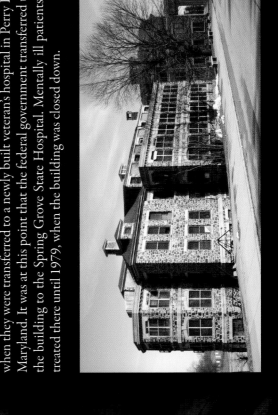

The Spring Grove State Hospital Center is the nation's second oldest psychiatric hospital. What started out in 1797 as a single hospital building has transformed now into a vast complex of buildings with various functions. Located in the center of the active campus is a building which was once known as the Foster-Wade Building. Originally entitled the Psychopathic Building, it was built in 1914 with federal funding to treat psychiatrically ill World War I serviceman. The World War I patients were treated there until 1925, when they were transferred to a newly built veteran's hospital in Perry Point, Maryland. It was at this point that the federal government transferred use of the building to the Spring Grove State Hospital. Mentally ill patients were treated there until 1979, when the building was closed down.

Pennhurst Hospital

Pennhurst, PA

At the time of its opening, in 1908, the organization was referred to as the Pennhurst Institution for the Feeble Minded and Epileptic. The excessive complex of buildings was once home to more than 3,550 patients and operated by 575 employees. Patients were put to work maintaining the facility, running shops, and other miscellaneous duties. The state was actually profiting from the facility. When the outside community found out about the inner workings of Pennhurst, many considered it nothing more than a grim warehouse for the mentally retarded. Investigations brought lawsuits against the institution, which was found guilty of violating patients' rights by way of abuse, sexual assault, isolation, and worse. The facility was forced to close in 1987 and has been vacant since. In 2010 the haunted attractions, Pennhurst Asylum and Tunnel Terror, opened at the site.

South Mountain Restoration Center

South Mountain, PA

Part of a much larger campus, this now vacant building at North Valley State Sanatorium was constructed in the 1930s at a cost of only $600,000. Known originally as the Children's Hospital, this building served as a preventorium for tuberculosis. The Children's Hospital's design was simple, consisting of two wings which jutted from a central pavilion. The building included two indoor pools intended specifically for tuberculosis patients, a library, four classrooms, exercise rooms, single patient rooms, an auditorium, a movie theatre, lounges, and a complete single-family house in the east wing for rehabilitation. The hospital opened in 1940 and operated as a preventorium until 1956. From 1956-1959 it provided a home for mentally retarded women. Later, from 1965-1985 the building housed geriatric patients. Finally, the building closed in 1985 primarily due to its deteriorating roof and has been sitting vacant since.

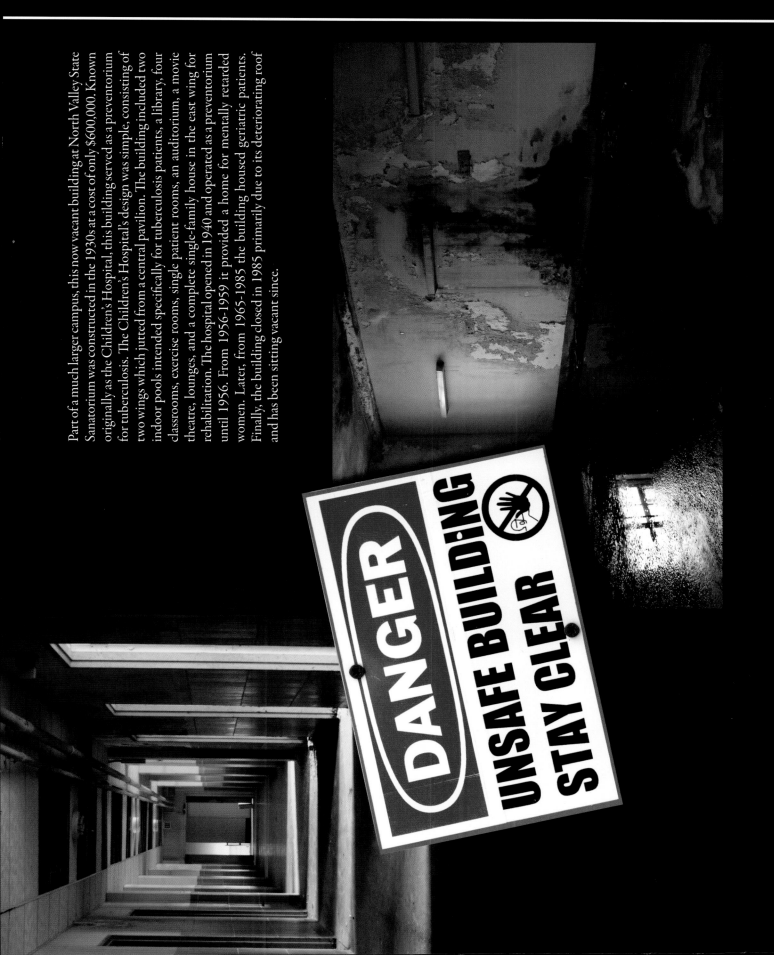

Forest Haven Asylum (also known as the DC Training School) was a mental retardation facility operated by the District. When it opened in the 1920s, Forest Haven had a reputation as a state-of-the-art treatment facility. The 250 acre compound was occupied by over 30 buildings—including cottages, a kitchen, theater, gym, a hydrotherapy building, and various other hospital and educational buildings. As time elapsed, Forest Haven's promising beginning crumbled and it became a dark and wretched place where the only way out for many of its morose patients was a tiny basement morgue which was the last stop before an unmarked grave on site. It has been reported that the very same graves are occasionally uncovered by flooding and erosion.

Forest Haven was closed in 1991 by the federal government after a lawsuit reported hundreds of incidents of abuse, neglect, molestation, and theft. There were also reports of experimental medical testing on helpless patients who were forced into trials as human guinea pigs.

Today, a handful of the buildings remain in use for education and rehabilitation but most of the site remains forlorn and rotting.

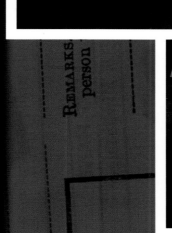

INDUSTRIAL

NO ENTRY WITHOUT PERMISSION

Persons willfully entering upon the premises shall, upon conviction, be deemed guilty of a misdemeanor, be punishable by imprisonment, fine or both.

Violators will be prosecuted under the provisions of Article 27, Section 541 & 542 of the Annotated Code of Maryland.

BALTIMORE GAS & ELECTRIC CO.

"It will neither bend, break nor burn."

–Thomas A. Edison

When the new Westport Power House began operating in 1906, it was said to be the "largest power station in the south" and the "largest reinforced concrete station in the world." Not a stick of wood was used in the construction, only reinforced concrete and steel—making it absolutely fireproof and virtually invincible to outside hazards. The original smokestack was 209 feet tall, making it the highest in Baltimore. Westport has undergone both evolutionary and revolutionary changes and expansions since its creation, powering Baltimore through the Great Depression and two world wars. The giant power station was closed down and was sealed up in 1993. After sitting vacant for nearly 15 years, the plant finally met its end through a massive demolition effort.

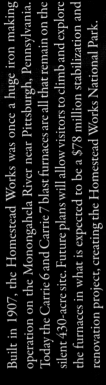

Built in 1907, the Homestead Works was once a huge iron making operation on the Monongahela River near Pittsburgh, Pennsylvania. Today the Carrie 6 and Carrie 7 blast furnaces are all that remain on the silent 430-acre site. Future plans will allow visitors to climb and explore the furnaces in what is expected to be a $78 million stabilization and renovation project, creating the Homestead Works National Park.

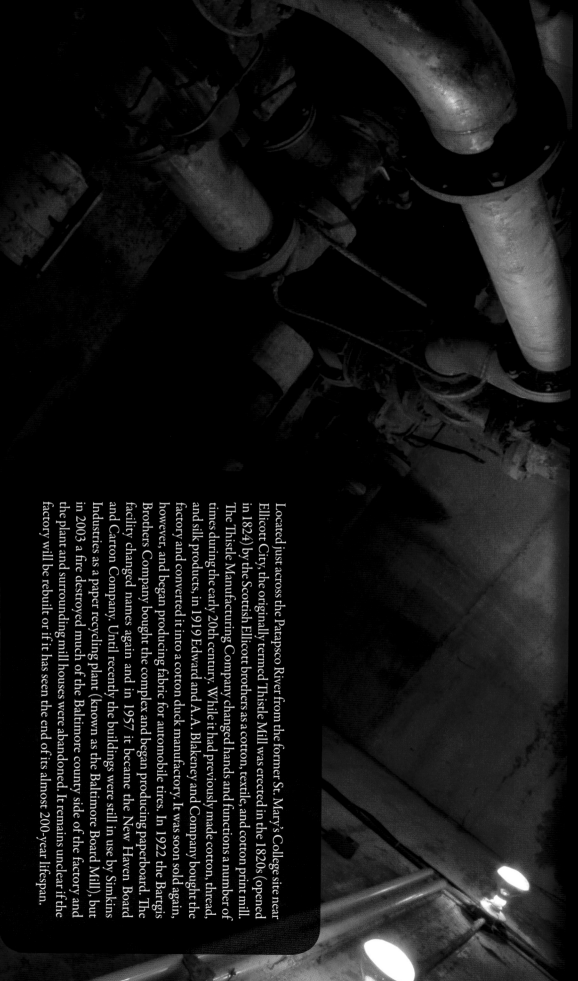

Thistle Mill

Ellicott City, MD

Located just across the Patapsco River from the former St. Mary's College site near Ellicott City, the originally termed Thistle Mill was erected in the 1820s (opened in 1824) by the Scottish Ellicott brothers as a cotton, textile, and cotton print mill. The Thistle Manufacturing Company changed hands and functions a number of times during the early 20th century. While it had previously made cotton, thread, and silk products, in 1919 Edward and A. A. Blakeney and Company bought the factory and converted it into a cotton duck manufactory. It was soon sold again, however, and began producing fabric for automobile tires. In 1922 the Bargis Brothers Company bought the complex and began producing paperboard. The facility changed names again and in 1957 it became the New Haven Board and Carton Company. Until recently the buildings were still in use by Simkins Industries as a paper recycling plant (known as the Baltimore Board Mill), but in 2003 a fire destroyed much of the Baltimore county side of the factory and the plant and surrounding mill houses were abandoned. It remains unclear if the factory will be rebuilt or if it has seen the end of its almost 200-year lifespan.

Bancroft Mill

Wilmington, DE

The now-massive Bancroft Mill complex started out as a diminutive paper mill in the late 1700s. The mill was the first in America to use an endless sheet machine, which would later revolutionize the manufacturing of paper. Consistently ravaged by fire and flood, the mill was rebuilt repeatedly until 1838 when the estate was sold. The property was purchased and converted into a cotton-spinning mill and by 1930 boasted the title of the largest cotton finishing works in the world. The mill housed various other mixed uses before closing down in 2003. Some of the buildings are currently being converted into condos while others are on a list waiting to be demolished.

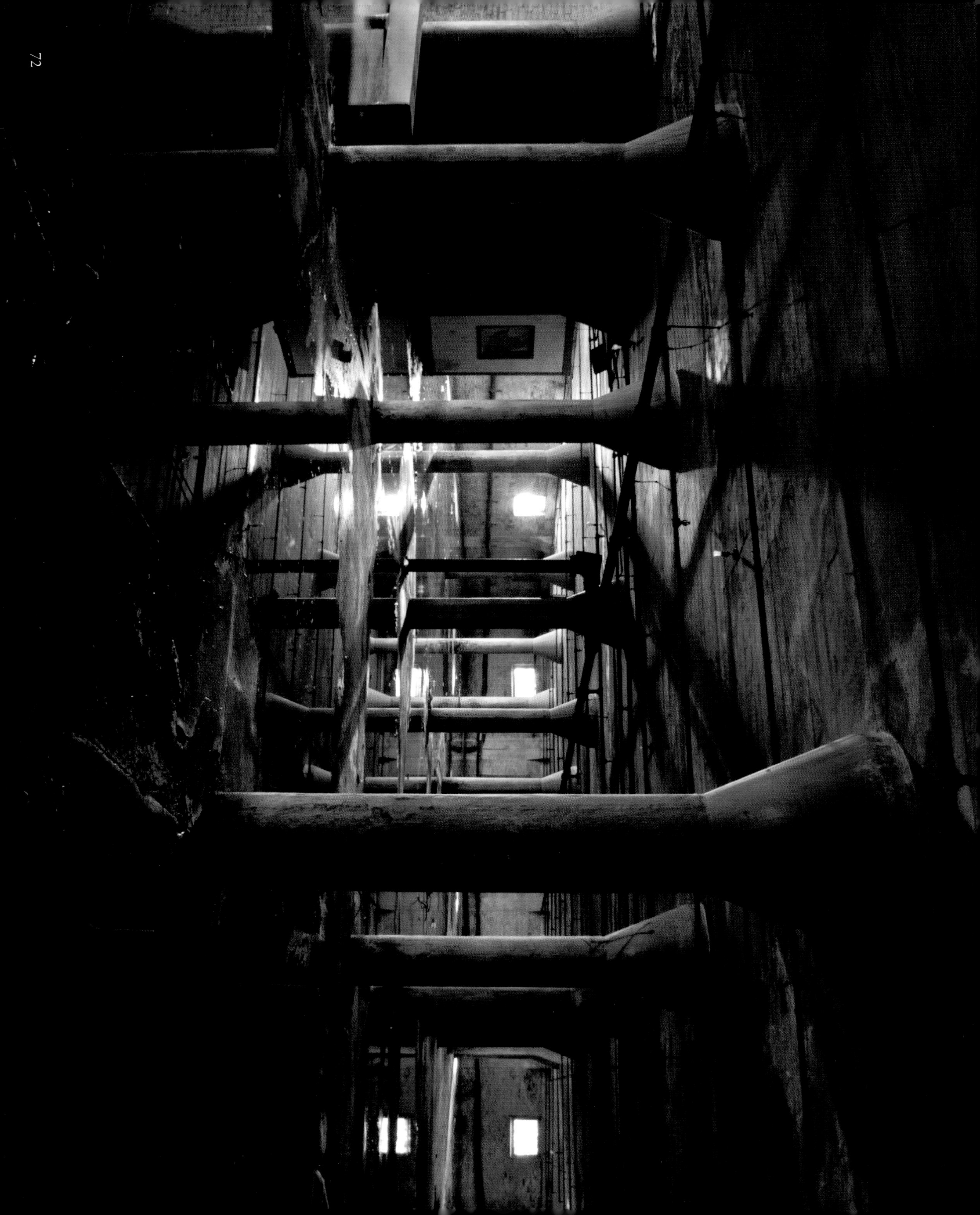

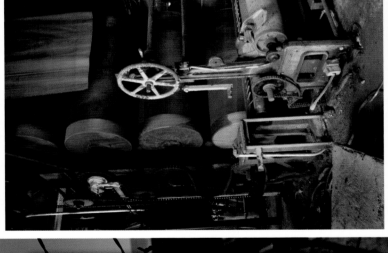

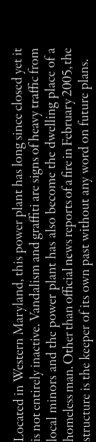

Located in Western Maryland, this power plant has long since closed yet it is not entirely inactive. Vandalism and graffiti are signs of heavy traffic from local minors and the power plant has also become the dwelling place of a homeless man. Other than official news reports of a fire in February 2005, the structure is the keeper of its own past without any word on future plans.

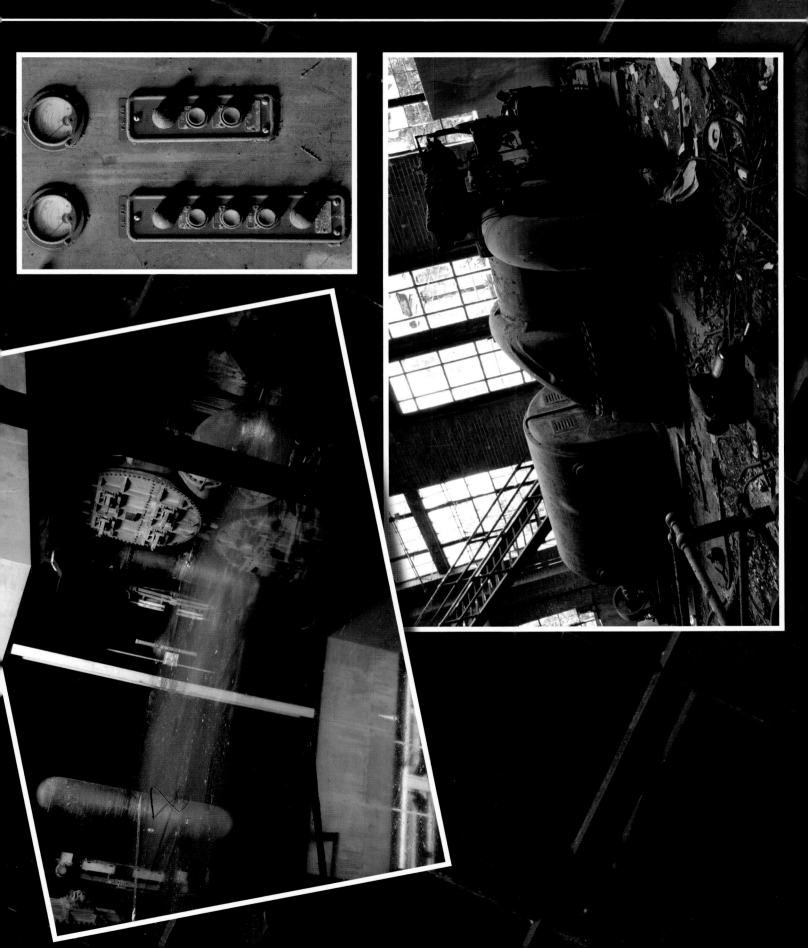

Phillips Packing Company

Cambridge, MD

Built in the early 1900s, Phillips Packing Company was at one time the largest employer in Cambridge, Maryland. One of Phillips' larger focuses was the vegetable canning business. In fact, their canning operation was so large that they did more canning than the Campbell Soup Company. After closing in the 1950s, the complex of factories and warehouses stood abandoned until a handful of them were converted to be used as a large antique shop. The still-abandoned portions of the site include a power building, warehouses, and other miscellaneous structures and equipment.

Belko Rubber Factory

Kingsville, MD

This is the site of an abandoned rubber factory hidden by a veil of forest in Kingsville, Maryland. Built in the 1960s, this factory passed through the hands of several owners before it was shut down for reasons yet to be determined (though asbestos contamination seems to be a strong hypothesis).

There has been evidence of fire since the closing of the factory (which is barely noticeable from the outside). "For-Sale" signs are posted on the property and it looks like someone has been working to clean the place up.

The American Brewery is not only a monument to the development of brewing, one of Baltimore's major industries, but also to the Germans who worked and lived in the area. John Frederick Wiessner, a German immigrant, leased the land in 1863 with the intention of erecting a brewery. Although there were already twenty-one breweries in Baltimore City and Baltimore County, Wiessner's Brewery rapidly expanded, employing many Germans who had been brewers or possessed knowledge of brewing prior to their emigration to America. In 1887 Wiessner constructed the present building to expand and modernize his brewery.

The height of the building and the internal organization of space were determined by the requirements of brewing, but its exuberant exterior reflects the tastes and decorative detail popular during the Victorian age in which it was built. The American Brewery was one of the largest and finest breweries in the state. The Wiessners were forced to sell during Prohibition, and the Allegheny Beverage Company was the last brewing company to occupy the brewery. In the mid-1930s, a modern brewery was created behind the old facade. American Beer was produced in this location until 1973.

The brewery was recently rehabilitated and is being used by Humanim, a non-profit organization serving individuals with disabilities.

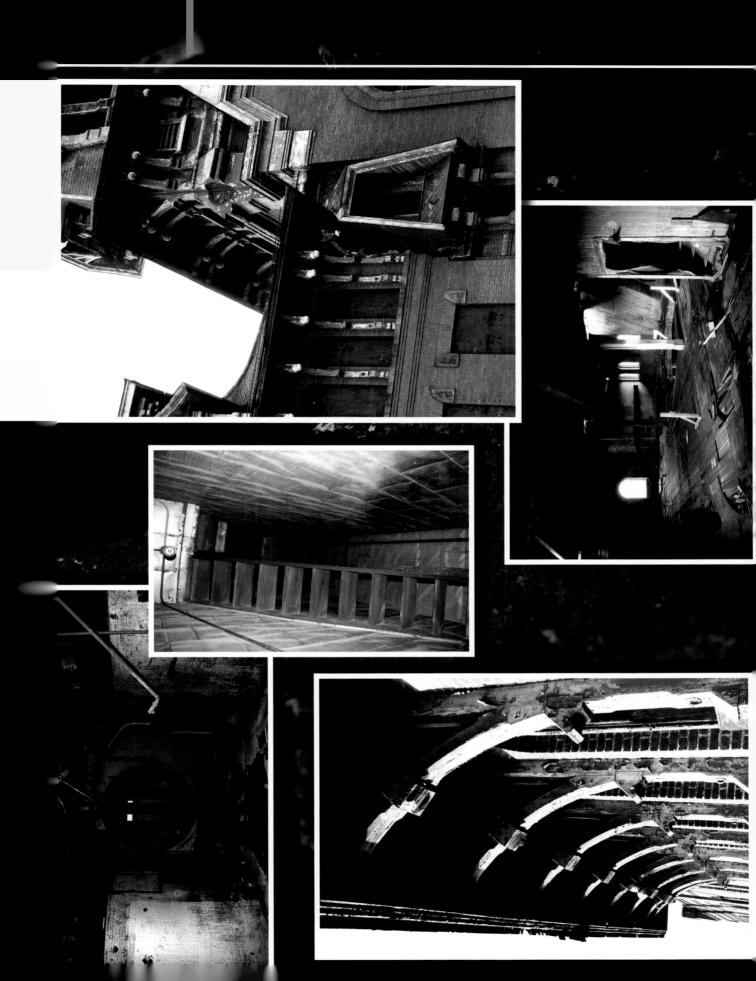

Located in the Brewers Hill area of Baltimore, the Gunther Brewery stands vacant, awaiting its inevitable transformation into mixed residential and commercial use structures. Dating back to the early 1900s, the property took its first steps as a beer brewing operation for the George Gunther, Jr. Brewing Company. While successful, Gunther was acquired by the larger Hamm's Brewing Company, who was in turn bought out by the F.& M. Schaefer Brewing Company. Both companies preserved the Gunther brands until the brewery was closed in 1978.

Lebow
Baltimore, MD

For three generations the Lebows carried on the family business as clothiers. The Baltimore factory produced and sold a wide range of clothing, though their main lines were coats and suits that could be found in luxury stores like Saks Fifth Avenue and Neiman Marcus. After closing its doors for over two decades, the racks are still filled with coats and hundreds of sewing machines line the factory floor. Five years ago the building's New York-based owner announced plans to move his marble cutting and polishing business into the empty building, but those plans never came to fruition. Current legal battles between the city and the owner leave the future of this building in question.

Richmond Power Station

Philadelphia, PA

The Richmond Power Station began generating electricity on the banks of the Delaware River in 1925. Richmond was a technological and architectural marvel with a grand exterior and a massive turbine hall. The 130 foot ceilings were shelter to many turbines, including the world's largest—a Westinghouse turbo-generator which was added in 1935. Since closing in 1985, the plant has stirred occasionally as a movie set for various television shows and films including *12 Monkeys*, *Transformers 2*, and *The Last Airbender*.

RELIGIOUS

St. Mary's College

Ilchester, MD

St. Mary's College—frequently referred to as Hell House—was originally named Mount Saint Clemens. A group calling themselves the Redemptorists started the religious school for boys in the mid 1800s. In 1882 a new chapel was built and encouragement from Pope Pius IX led the Redemptorists to change the name of the school to Saint Mary's College.

The Redemptorists continued to operate the school until 1972, when it closed due to a decline in enrollment. In 1987 the land was split up and sold to the state and to a private investor.

Throughout this period of the school's vacant existence, Allen Hudson acted as the caretaker for the property. Hudson maintained the property to the best of his ability—working full time chasing off thrill seekers and vandals. Hudson was well known by the local trespassers as the mean old man with the rottweilers and a shotgun. Hudson was even charged with assault, battery, and assault with the intent to murder in 1996, when he shot and critically wounded a trespasser. It is not known what became of the charges against him but Hudson remained caretaker and continued living on the property.

On Halloween night in 1997, vandals burned down the main building. The brick walls still left standing after the inferno were unstable and a threat to Hudson's stone home. The caretaker was forced by police to vacate the property. The ruins have since been totally demolished.

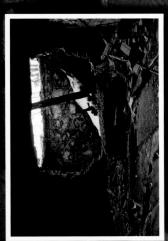

Its foundation laid in 1880, the Ammendale Normal Institute was said to contain the largest buildings in Prince George's County at the time. The institute was started by an organization called the Christian Brothers, a Roman Catholic teaching order. Also on the property is St. Joseph's Chapel, a freestanding Queen Anne-style church. In front of the church is a very interesting apse-like monument or shrine of some sort constructed from volcanic rock and sea shells. It probably once displayed a statue of Mary, St. Joseph, or some other saint related to the organization. The institute was destroyed by fire in 1998 and the surrounding structures were closed up. An active cemetery is still on site and the grounds continue to be maintained.

John Wesley United Methodist

Abingdon, MD

The John Wesley United Methodist Church is located along Philadelphia Road in Abingdon, Maryland. The church was given to African Americans by Quakers in approximately 1868. In addition to religious services, the church was also used as a school before a newer building was built nearby for this very purpose. Also located on the property is a dilapidated parsonage, a cemetery with some weathered headstones, and an old wooden outhouse. As of recently, the roof has fallen in and the entire structure has been demolished.

Saints Peter and Paul

Pittsburgh, PA

The Saints Peter and Paul Church was established as a German parish in 1857 but it was not until the late 1880s that construction began on the current building. The cornerstone of the church was laid in 1857. Construction endured for two years and the completed church was dedicated on November 26, 1859. In 1909 the building was gutted by a fire after being struck by lightning. The parish rebuilt a new church which incorporated the remains of the old church—including the stone walls, twin towers, and the alter. Construction of the new church was completed in late 1910. By the end of the twentieth century Pittsburgh's population had declined, and with a general dwindling of interest in modern religion, the city could no longer support the number of independent parishes in existence. In 1992 Saints Peter and Paul merged with five other parishes to form the new St. Charles Lwanga parish. The Church closed after the merger and was later sold. The building currently sits vacant with an undetermined future.

Transfiguration of Our Lord

Philadelphia, PA

An unfortunate and ironic title considering the building's lack of reflection on Christ's transfiguration from a man into the son of God. It has instead fallen gradually from a late-gothic style beauty into a neighborhood garbage depository, and now finally, fallen to the fated wrecking ball. After 95 years of service, this church had sat vacant since 2000. The structure is comprised of an upper church in the standard Western European layout (though with a relatively shortened transept), which provides seating for about 1,000 people while a basement level church seats approximately 400 people. Also located on the property is a three-story rectory, the former convent, and a three-story school building.

MILITARY

Fort Carroll is a fortified 3.4-acre artificial island located on the Patapsco River just south of Baltimore's Key Bridge. The fort was built to replace Fort McHenry which was located too close to the growing city to provide adequate protection. Construction began sometime around 1847 and remained incomplete through the Civil War—during which advances in artillery rendered the fort's defenses obsolete. In the late 1890s, the fort was rearmed and updated to the Endicott System (a program designed to improve and rearm U.S. coastal defenses) in response to hostilities with Spain; but it never saw war. In 1921 the army left the fort abandoned until returning to limited service during World War II, acting as a firing range for the Army and Coast Guard, as well as a checkpoint for ships entering the harbor. After World War II the fort and lighthouse were again abandoned.

The property has since been passed from one developer to the next—all with failed attempts at creating a new use for the old fort. In this time the complex has descended from functionality into a jungle-like habitat for thousands of birds.

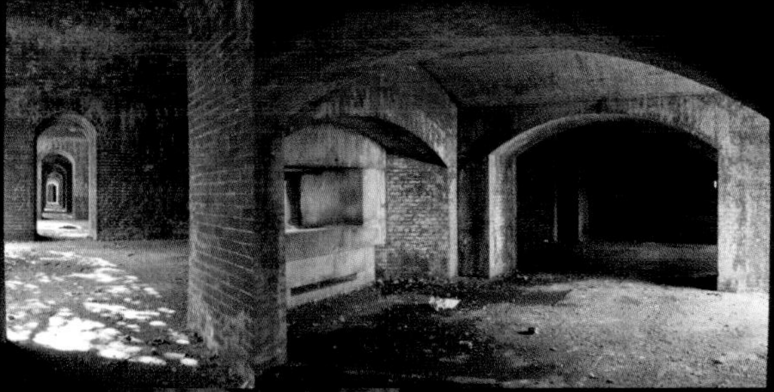
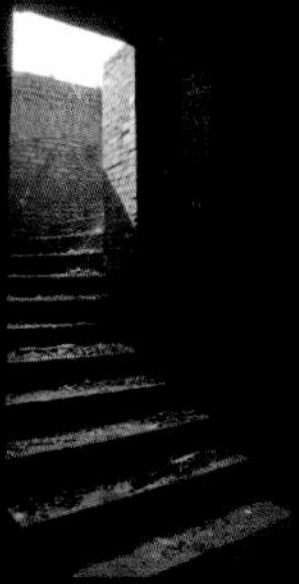
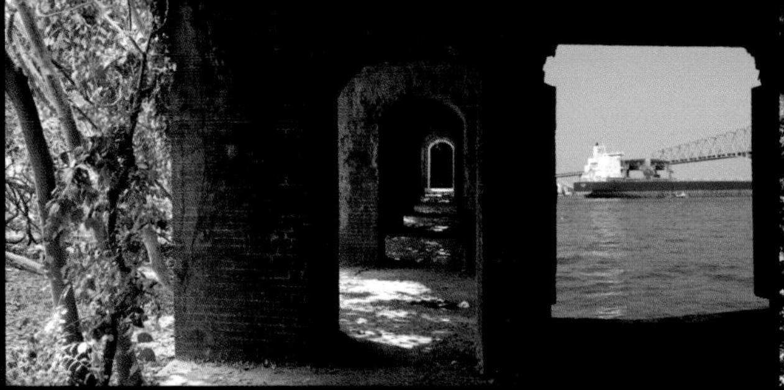
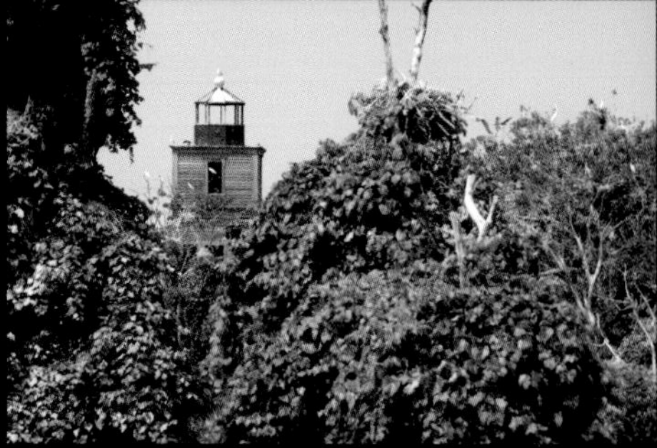
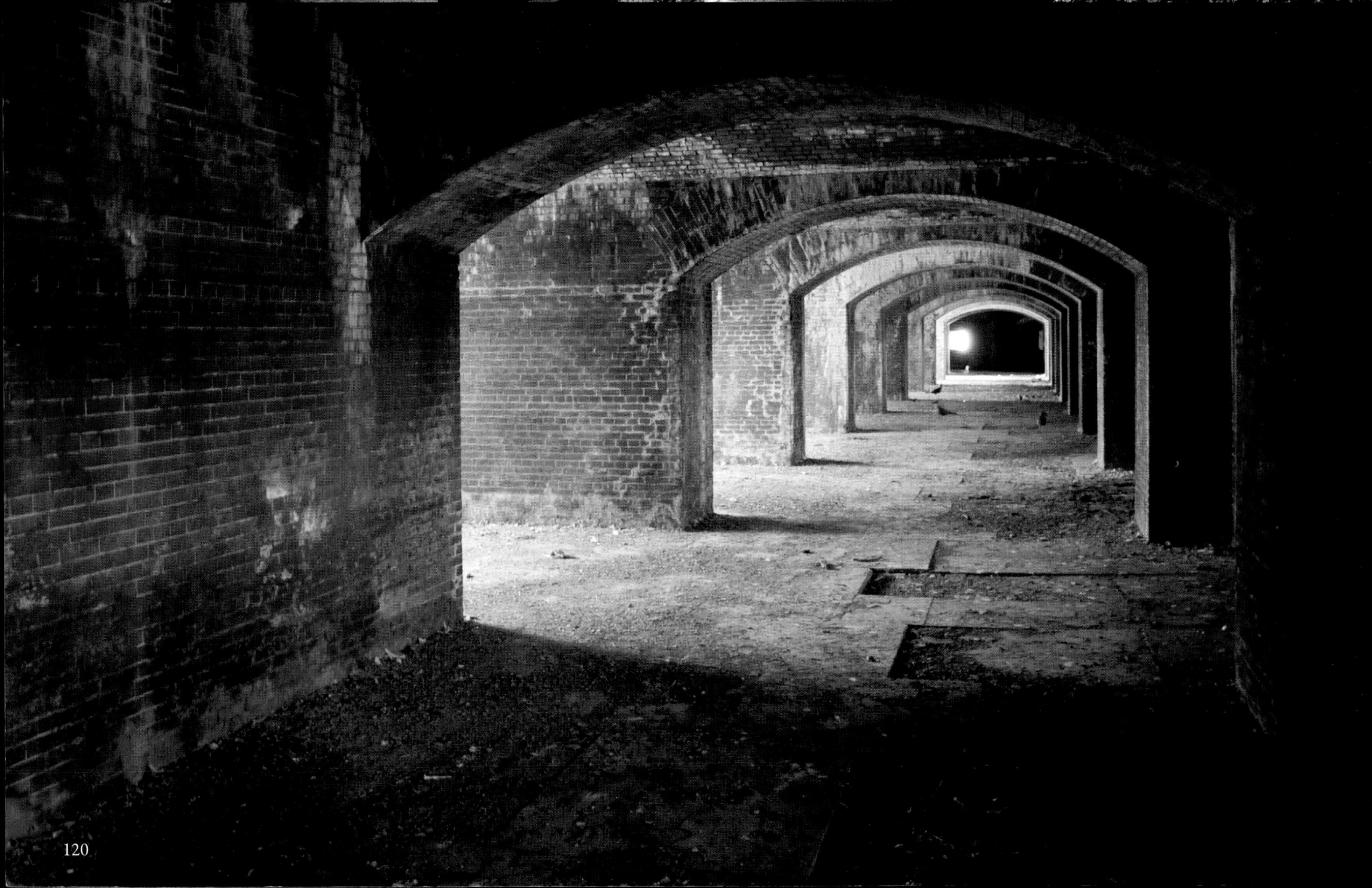

Nike Launch Site BA-09

Fork, MD

The Nike (named after the winged Greek goddess of victory) was the title given to a program that produced the world's first successful guided surface-to-air missiles. During the start of the Cold War, the United States camouflaged Nike missile sites within populated areas under the threat of a new wave of Soviet long range bomber aircraft, which were capable of carrying bombs well within the continental US.

This Launch Control Area (LCA) site envelopes approximately 10 acres. On site is a guardhouse, former barracks, water tanks, pump house, an acid-neutralization pit, three missile silos, three monitoring wells, and numerous trailers, autos, and other miscellaneous skeletons of discarded military objects. In 1954, the United States Government obtained the land for this Nike Launch site from a private owner. The site formerly contained the equipment required to assemble, test, and maintain missiles and associated launchers. According to the current owner, in 1962, the site was deactivated because it was unsuitable for the Hercules missile system that began deployment that year. Between 1962 and 1985, the site was inactive, but the property was still owned by the federal government. In 1985 a neighboring farmer purchased the property from the federal government for $65,000. Then, for a short time in 1986, the property was leased to the County Police Department. Since that time, the property has seen continued use from the farmer.

This site is on the State Master List, which identifies potential hazardous waste sites in Maryland. For this reason it has limited possibilities for any useful functions and rests piled with junk and claimed by nature. The site barely resembles the military facility it used to be. The watch towers are gone and the access doors to the silos have been welded shut. Other access points have been secured with pad-locks.

Forts Armistead & Howard

During the Spanish-American War the only naval defense for Baltimore was the famous Fort McHenry; accredited with its fame during the War of 1812, when the Americans fought the British in the Battle of Baltimore and Francis Scott Key penned "The Star-Spangled Banner." Nearly 100 years later the fort had been rendered useless for naval defense. In 1901 Congress created the U.S. Army Coastal Artillery Corps (CAC). The CAC was responsible for establishing a new harbor defense for Baltimore, and to do so they built a network of forts to protect the city's Inner Harbor. Two of these forts were Fort Howard (also known as the Fort at North Point) and Fort Armistead (also known as Hawkins Point). These forts were futilely garrisoned with troops and anti-ship cannons which never saw any wartime action. As time progressed, the defenses became antiquated and thus useless against advancing military weaponry, so the forts were limited to training or ammo storage only. The facilities were later stripped down and now serve as public parks.

Naval Training Center

Port Deposit, MD

The United States Naval Training Center (USNTC Bainbridge) was located on the bluffs of the Susquehanna River in Port Deposit, Maryland. The 1,100-acre site was once engrossed by over 500 buildings and 55,000 people. The NTC was built in 1942 as a training center for World War II recruits. When the war was over, the facility was deactivated but reopened in 1951 in reaction to the Korean War crisis. After the war the NTC became home to various schools and uses — including the Naval Preparatory School, the Nuclear Power School, the Naval Reserve Manpower Center, WAVES Headquarters, and a U.S. Naval Hospital. The NTC closed in 1976. Only a handful of buildings remain on the barren site.

NRL Satellite Facility

During the 1960s an experimental satellite communications facility was built by the Naval Research Laboratory (NRL) in Accokeek, Maryland, at former Nike missile base W-45. The site was equipped for satellite tracking, data processing, and various communications experiments. One of the primary uses of the facility was a project called Compass Link. Compass Link was established during the Vietnam War to transfer high priority photos between Vietnam and Washington, DC. The facility was also heavily involved in the testing/development of commercial and defense satellites—the MILSTAR program and the FLTSATCOM program. In the late 1990s, the facility was decommissioned and auctioned off to a private investor. Everything at the site has been totally demolished.

130

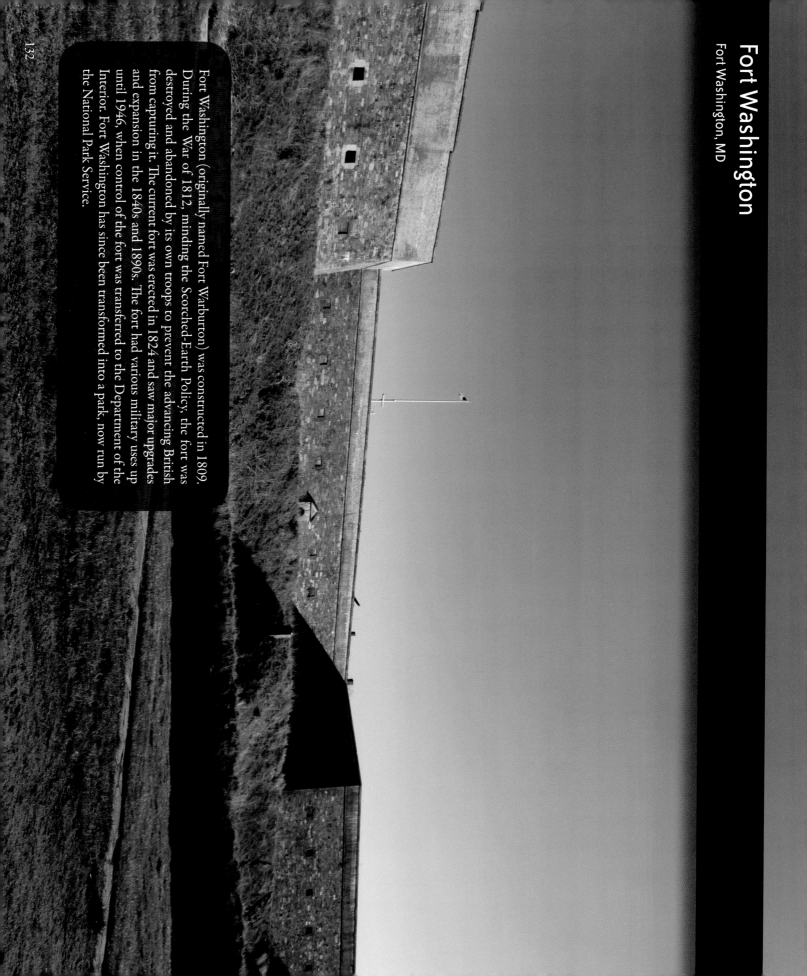

Fort Washington

Fort Washington, MD

Fort Washington (originally named Fort Warburton) was constructed in 1809. During the War of 1812, minding the Scorched-Earth Policy, the fort was destroyed and abandoned by its own troops to prevent the advancing British from capturing it. The current fort was erected in 1824 and saw major upgrades and expansion in the 1840s and 1890s. The fort had various military uses up until 1946, when control of the fort was transferred to the Department of the Interior. Fort Washington has since been transformed into a park, now run by the National Park Service.

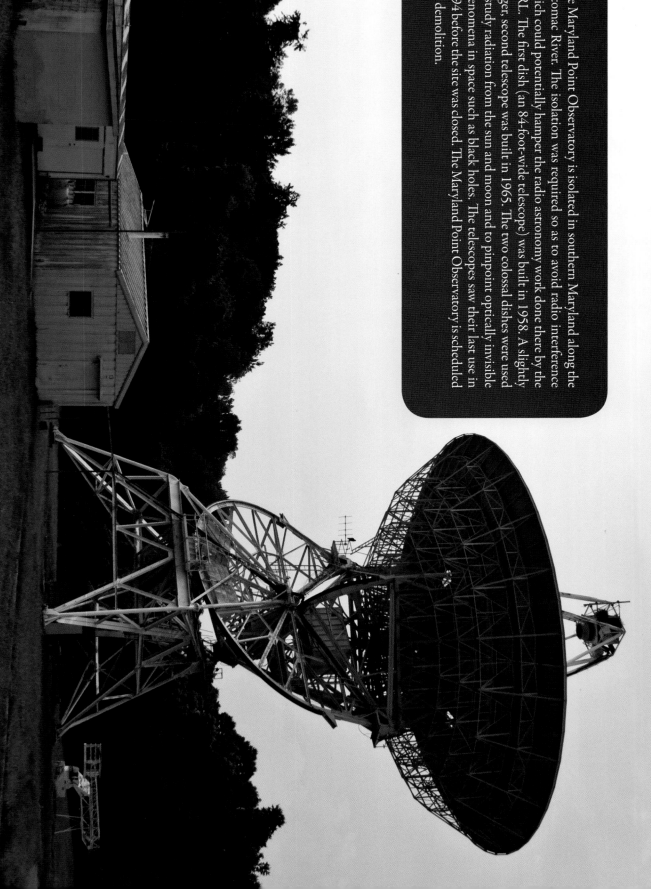

Maryland Point Observatory

Maryland Point, MD

The Maryland Point Observatory is isolated in southern Maryland along the Potomac River. The isolation was required so as to avoid radio interference which could potentially hamper the radio astronomy work done there by the NRL. The first dish (an 84-foot-wide telescope) was built in 1958. A slightly larger, second telescope was built in 1965. The two colossal dishes were used to study radiation from the sun and moon and to pinpoint optically invisible phenomena in space such as black holes. The telescopes saw their last use in 1994 before the site was closed. The Maryland Point Observatory is scheduled for demolition.

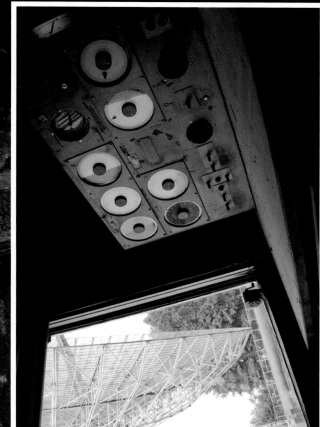

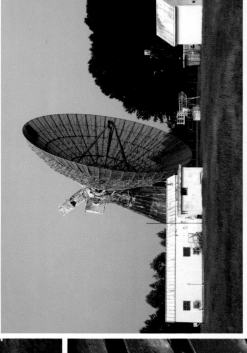

EDUCATION

The deserted buildings of the former Tome School for Boys sit atop a 200-foot bluff overlooking the Susquehanna River. The school established its roots in 1901 with a building known as The Inn. As many as sixteen more buildings were erected, including Memorial Hall which was designed to be the awe-inspiring focal point of the entire campus. Other buildings included dormitories, a dining hall, gym, indoor pool, power plant, and master cottages. The Tome School was hit hard during the depression, and with declining class populations failed to produce profits. In 1941 the Navy purchased the school and used it as a Naval Academy Preparatory School during World War II and the Korean Conflict. In the 1980s the site functioned for a short time as a Job Corps training facility.

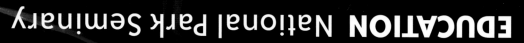

The National Park Seminary, also known as The Seminary at Forest Glen, is located in Silver Spring, Maryland. The site history dates back to the 1700s, when the area was occupied by a tobacco plantation. A portion of the land was later sold and an inn was built in 1887. At the time the area was not easy to access from the District and the hotel suffered financially. In an effort to revive the inn it was converted into a casino with gambling and bars, but the idea did not reap necessary profits. In 1894 the property was leased and the casino was converted into a finishing school for girls. Hard times during the depression damaged enrollment and the primary focus of the school transformed from training the affluent elite to a college that all could benefit from — emphasizing academics and practical trade skills which improved employability. Soon after, the United States entered World War II and the property was seized by the Army to use for treatment and recovery of wounded soldiers returning to the states. The property was known as the Walter Reed Army Medical Center during this era. In 2004 ownership of the property was transferred to developers. The buildings at the site have since been converted to luxury condominiums.

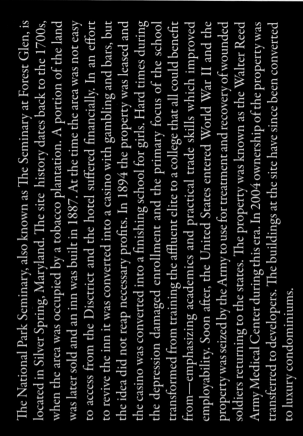

The Northeast Manual Training School (also known as Edison High School) is located in a notoriously violent, drug-ravaged part of North Philadelphia known as the Badlands. When it closed sometime around 2000, the school was ranked as the worst middle school in the city. It was not always that way though... The school was built in 1903 as one of the first vocational schools in the area—a prototype design that future schools would follow. The well-known school saw great success in preparing students for careers in area industries. After the vocational school relocated out of the area, the school endured several uses and name changes. As the area worsened, the school fell into corruption and neglect before the city eventually shut it down. The fate of this forlorn castle is unknown.

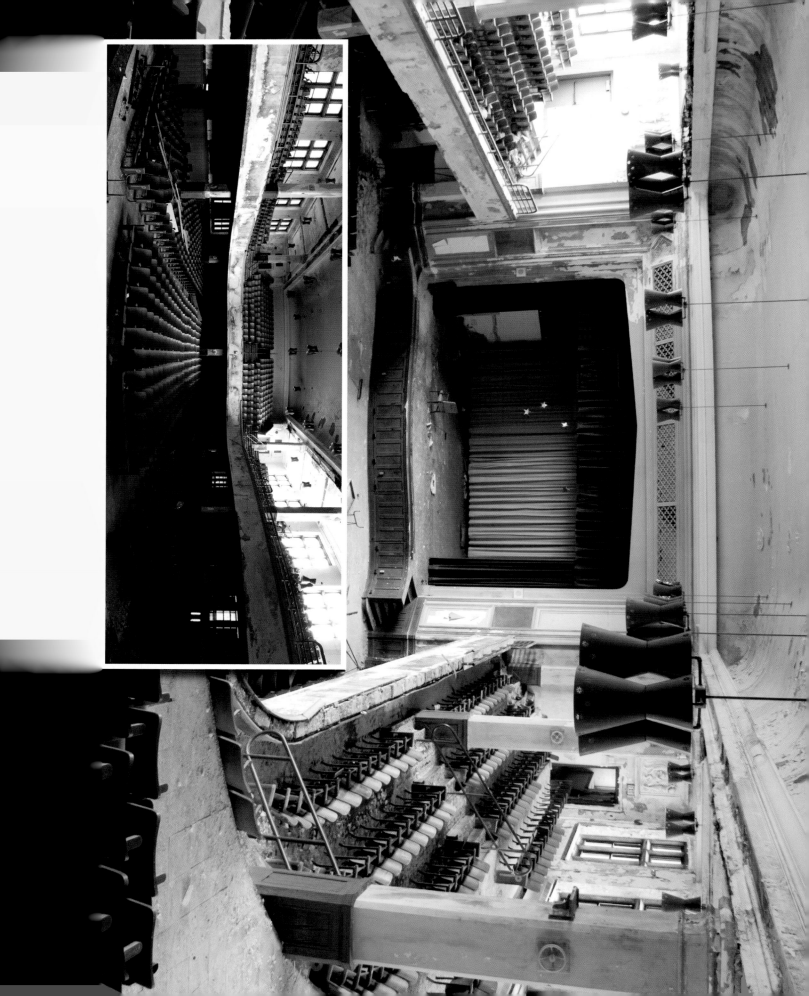

ENTERTAINMENT

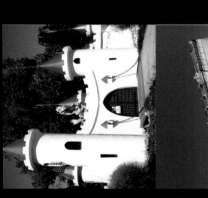

Mayfair Theatre

Baltimore, MD

The Mayfair Theatre has been around since the 1870s. The structure was originally known as the Natatorium. It housed a subterranean spa with Turkish baths, steam rooms, and what was once the city's largest swimming pool. There is still evidence of the baths and steam rooms hidden away in the basement of the theatre. The structure was later converted into a movie house and is now the oldest standing movie theatre in the city. The theatre closed up in the 1980s and has been sealed up since. When taking a look at the front facade, the theatre appears to be in good standing, but sometime during the 1990s weather and neglect tightened their grip on the building and the roof collapsed, destroying most of the interior structure.

Ghost Ferry

Baltimore, MD

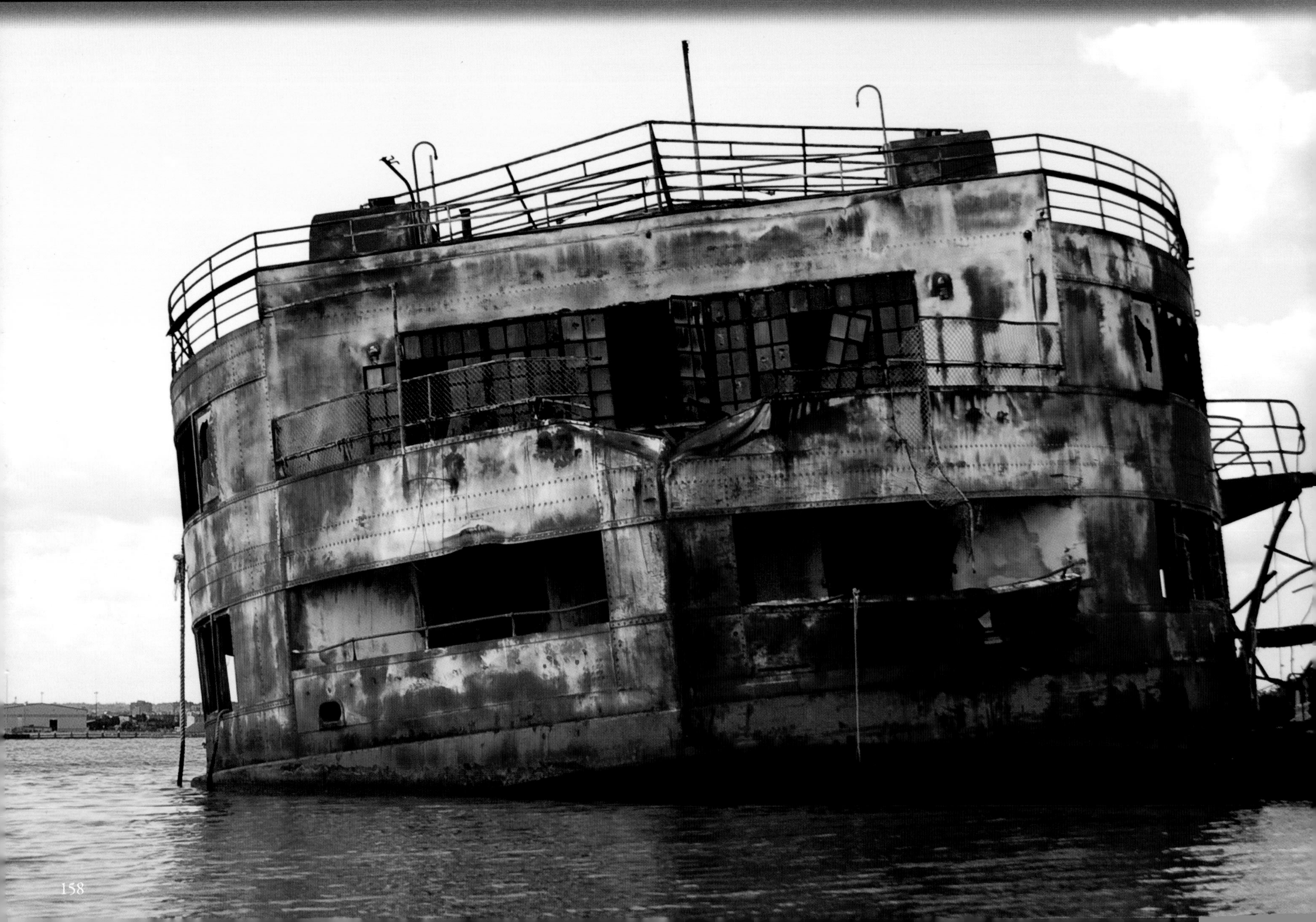

This vessel was stranded in Baltimore's Patapsco River near what used to be a ship breaking site where ships were dismantled for scrap metal. Little could be found to identify the ship or its origins but judging by the open decks, dance floors, bars, and central ballroom this was one big floating party. The Ghost Ferry was cut into scrap metal and shipped away on a barge.

CORRECTIONS

Lorton Prison

Lorton, VA

Lorton Prison started out as a small workhouse in 1910, when there was a common belief that a prisoner's hard work and learned skills, combined with fresh air, would turn him into a model citizen. The prison started out with a capacity of 60 inmates and over time grew to an extensive 3,200-acre complex which housed over 7,000 inmates. Operating at nearly 50% over capacity and understaffed, the prison became an exceedingly dangerous place—there were numerous reports of murder and uncontrollable drug trafficking inside. A lack of funding forced Lorton to close in 2001. Since closing no time has been wasted to reuse the property. Residential housing and a school has been built just beside the old prison buildings. Other future plans may include art studios, a museum, golf course expansion, residential housing, a retirement home, a cemetery, and park land.

Charles H. Hickey, Jr. School

Baltimore, MD

Built around 1910, the Maryland School for Boys was created in an effort to separate children from adult criminals. The complex cared for and treated approximately 300 delinquent boys and young men between the ages of 15 and 17. It served as a detention center for youth awaiting trial and also as a training school for youth committed by the court. In 1985 the school changed its name to the Charles H. Hickey, Jr. School in honor of a former Baltimore County sheriff. As facility conditions and "quality of life" deteriorated, the governor announced that Hickey be closed in 2005, but years later the facility remains in operation. The photos only show the areas no longer in use.

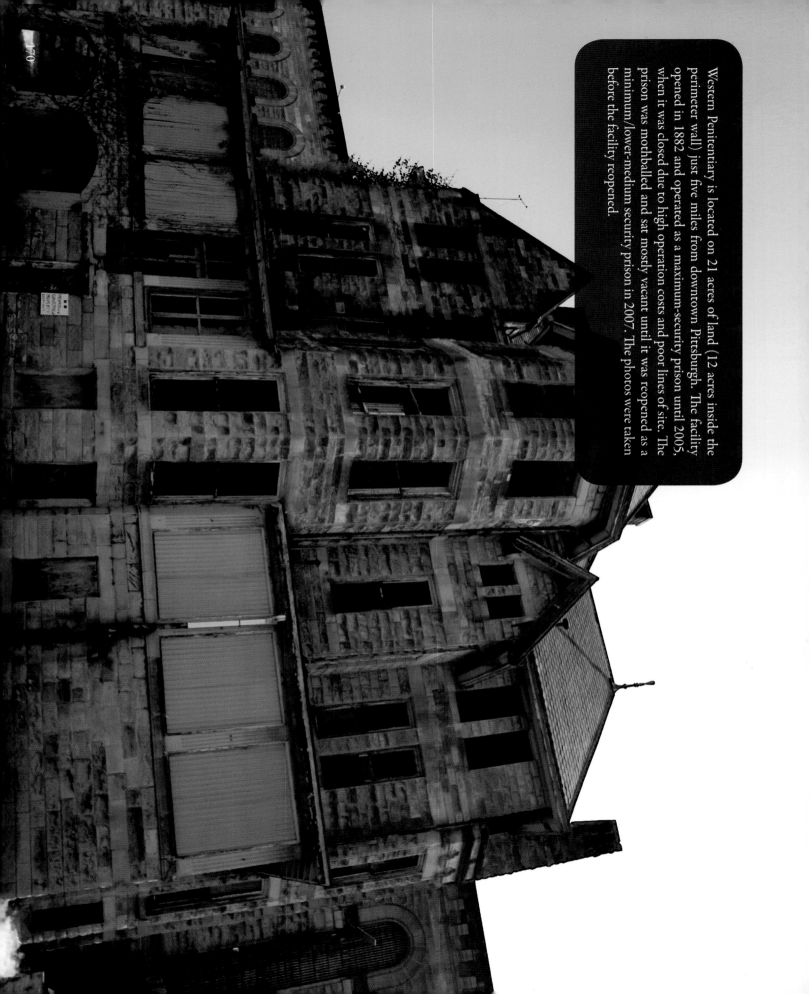

Western Penitentiary is located on 21 acres of land (12 acres inside the perimeter wall) just five miles from downtown Pittsburgh. The facility opened in 1882 and operated as a maximum-security prison until 2005, when it was closed due to high operation costs and poor lines of site. The prison was mothballed and sat mostly vacant until it was reopened as a minimum/lower-medium security prison in 2007. The photos were taken before the facility reopened.

MISCELLANEOUS

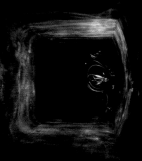

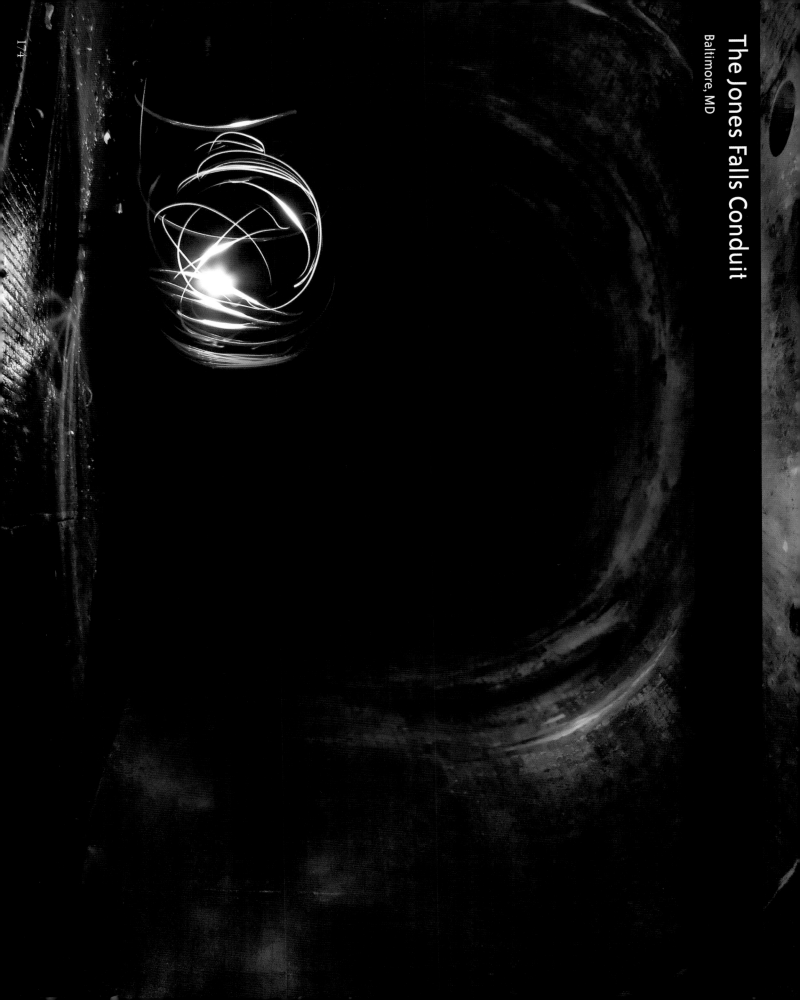

The Jones Falls Conduit

Baltimore, MD

In the early 1700s, flooding and waterborne disease were substantial problems that slowed the growth of Baltimore. To solve the problem, engineers came up with a plan that would bury the area streams and rivers in a system of underground storm drain. The Jones Falls Conduit is one of those systems. The Jones Falls watershed encompasses approximately 58 square miles of Baltimore County. It drains into a stream and runs alongside the Jones Falls Expressway (I-83) until it descends underground near North Howard Street. Once underground, the stream passes through a massive concrete and brick conduit, traveling in total darkness for about 1.7 miles before it outfalls into Baltimore's Inner Harbor.

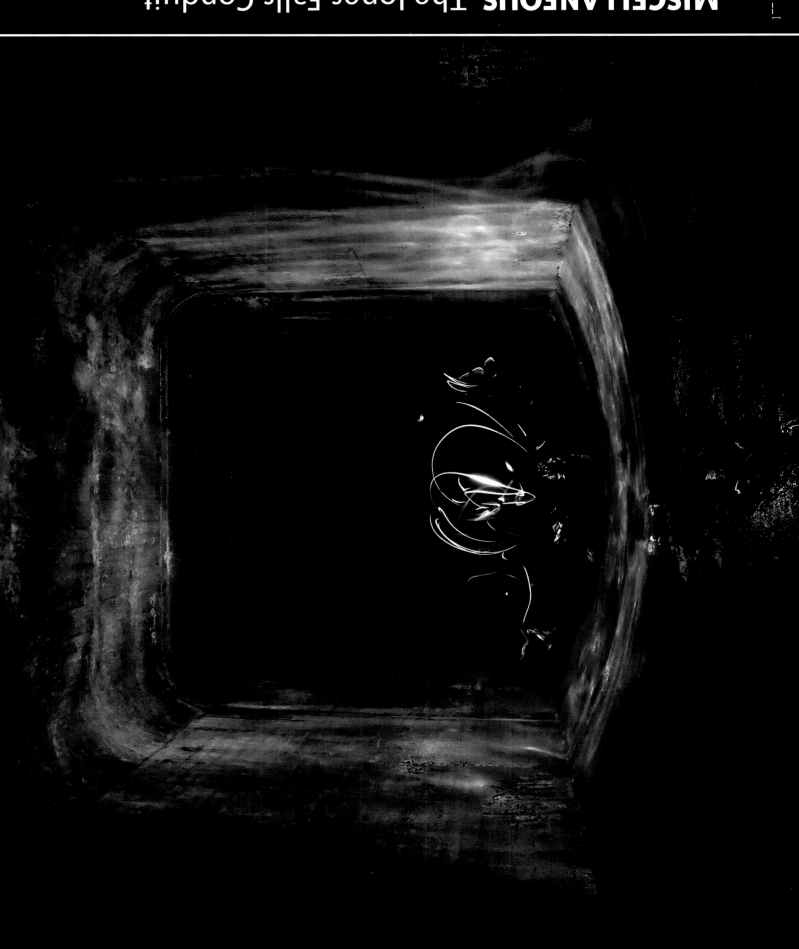

B & O Railroad Grain Terminal

Baltimore, MD

178

Fort Pitt Steel Casting Co.
Pittsburgh, PA

Vane Brothers Co.
Baltimore, MD

Tank Cleaning Ship
Baltimore, MD

Living quarters at former Seton Psychiatric Institute
Baltimore, MD

USS Sanctuary Baltimore, MD

St. Mark's Baltimore, MD

Unknown Church Baltimore, MD

Schenuit Rubber Baltimore, MD

Wiley Cork Co. Wilmington, DE

Misc. Industrial Site Baltimore, MD